The Primary Source Library of the Thirteen Colonies and the Lost Colony™

The Colony of Connecticut

A Primary Source History

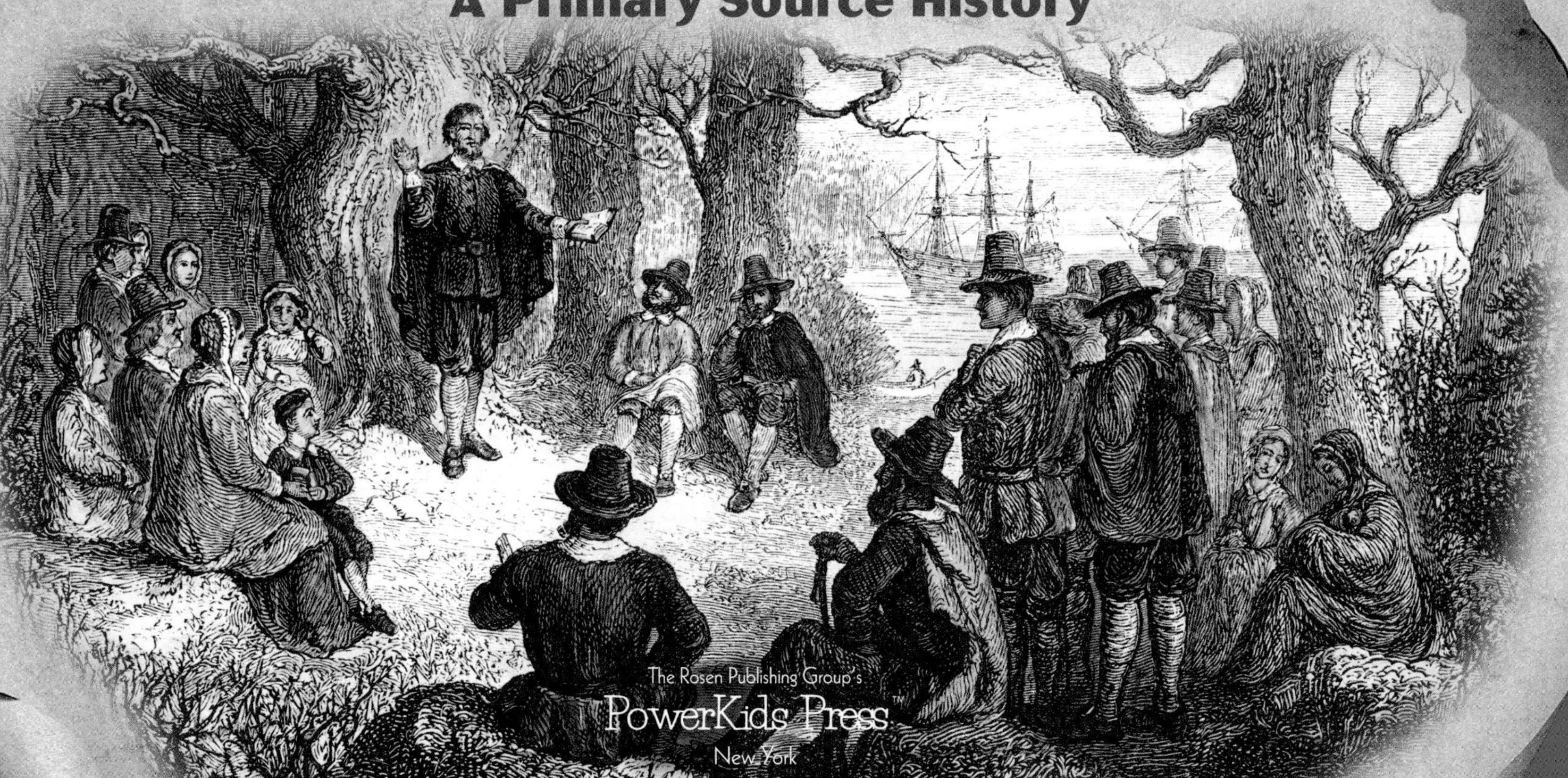

The Rosen Publishing Group's
PowerKids Press™
New York

Jake Miller

Published in 2006 by The Rosen Publishing Group, Inc.
29 East 21st Street, New York, NY 10010

First Edition

Editor: Jennifer Way
Book Design: Ginny Chu

Photo Credits: Cover, p. 20 © North Wind Picture Archives; p. 4 Courtesy of the John Carter Brown Library, Brown University, Providence, RI; p. 4 (inset) © Corbis; p. 5 Copyright © 2004, Mashantucket Pequot Museum & Research Center. All rights reserved; p. 6 © The New York Public Library/Art Resource, NY; p. 6 (inset) © Massachusetts Historical Society, Boston, MA, USA/The Bridgeman Art Library; p. 8 © Mashantucket Pequot Museum and Research Center, Archives & Special Collections, MSS52; p. 8 (inset) © Cynthia (Frégeau) Abbott; p. 10, Library of Congress Prints and Photograph Division, HABS CONN,6-NEWLO, 1–4; p. 10 (inset) Rare Books Division, The New York Public Library, Astor, and Tilden Foundations; p. 12 © John Hammond/NTPL/The Image Works; p. 12 (inset) Museum of Connecticut History; pp. 13, 16 © Getty Images; p. 14 © Bettmann/Corbis; p. 14 (inset) Library of Congress; p. 16 (inset) © Mary Evans Picture Library; p. 18 © Atwater Kent Museum of Philadelphia/Bridgeman Art Library; p. 18 (inset) National Archives and Records Administration; p. 20 (inset) © The Art Archive/National Archives, Washington DC.

Library of Congress Cataloging-in-Publication Data

Miller, Jake, 1969–
The colony of Connecticut : a primary source history / Jake Miller.
p. cm. — (The primary source library of the thirteen colonies and the Lost Colony)
Includes bibliographical references and index.
ISBN 1-4042-3030-0 (library binding)
1. Connecticut—History—Colonial period, ca. 1600–1775—Juvenile literature. 2. Connecticut—History—1775–1865—Juvenile literature. I. Title.

F97.M55 2006
974.6'02—dc22

2004021843

Manufactured in the United States of America

Contents

This map of Long Island Sound and the Connecticut coast, above, was created around 1679. Inset: John Cabot was born Giovanni Caboto in Italy around 1450. After his journey to North America, he went on another journey in which he attempted to reach Japan. He is believed to have been lost at sea in 1499.

Finding Connecticut

The land that became the Connecticut Colony was located in the Connecticut River valley and along the north shore of Long Island Sound. Before Europeans settled Connecticut, the Pequot and the Mohegan Native Americans already lived there.

The first European to see the mainland of North America was an Italian sailor named John Cabot. Cabot sailed for England and claimed the mainland of North America for that country in 1497. The first European to find the Connecticut River was a Dutch explorer named Adriaen Block. He sailed up the river in 1614.

The Pequot and the Mohegan Native Americans are thought to have come to the area known as Connecticut around 1500. It is believed that these groups came to the area from near Lake Champlain, in New York. This Pequot necklace, above, was created in the seventeenth century.

The picture above shows Thomas Hooker leading settlers from near Boston, Massachusetts, to where they would found the town of Hartford, Connecticut. The Connecticut Colony took its name from the Pequot word "Quinnehtukqut," which means "land along the great tidal river." Inset: John Winthrop Jr., who founded Saybrook, Connecticut, was born in 1606.

Settling New England and Connecticut

In 1620, the first successful English colony in New England was founded in Plymouth, Massachusetts. This was followed by the Massachusetts Bay Colony in 1630. England could not afford to pay for colonies, so the king let private companies make the **investment** and take the chance instead. The founders of these colonies in Massachusetts were Puritans.

Once they had started towns around Plymouth and Boston, some of the Puritans needed more land for farming. In 1636, Thomas Hooker brought 100 settlers and 160 cattle from near Boston, Massachusetts, to found the town of Hartford on the Connecticut River. That same year John Winthrop Jr. began building a fort in Saybrook. These early settlements joined to form the Connecticut Colony in 1665.

The picture above is a Pequot fort near Mystic, Connecticut. It was published in Newes from America by John Underhill in 1638. Underhill and John Mason had led an attack on this fort in 1637. Inset: Lion Gardiner built the Colonial fort in Saybrook. He helped guard the fort during the Pequot War. This statue of Gardiner is located in Saybrook.

The Pequot War

As the settlers came to Connecticut, they made plans to grow the colony. There was one problem, though. Native American groups, such as the Pequot, already lived in these nearby areas.

The Pequot did not want the English to move into their territory. In 1636, fighting known as the Pequot War broke out between the two groups. It was the first war between settlers and Native Americans in New England. The leaders of the Massachusetts colonies and Connecticut sent troops.

In 1637, a group of Connecticut settlers led by Captain John Underhill and Captain John Mason attacked a Pequot town while the town's warriors were away. The settlers crept up on the town early in the morning and set it on fire. Only about 12 of nearly 700 Pequots lived through the attack.

The mill in the above picture was built around 1650 on John Winthrop Jr.'s land. Inset: *This is the coat of arms for John Underhill's family. It appears in his 1638 book* Newes from America. *A coat of arms is a group of images that stands for a family.*

Building the Connecticut Colony

The first English settlers in Connecticut were farmers, but the colonists soon began to look for other ways to make a living. Along the coast there were successful fishing businesses. Connecticut also had a growing shipbuilding trade. After John Winthrop Jr. started the settlement at Saybrook in 1635, he went to England to learn about business and to find investors. When he returned he built mills and factories, including plants to make gunpowder. Soon Connecticut mills were producing shoes, woolen cloth, and candles.

In 1638, wealthy Puritans founded New Haven as a colony separate from the Connecticut Colony. Its natural harbor on Long Island Sound made it an excellent place for trade and shipping. In 1665, New Haven joined the Connecticut Colony.

From the Fundamental Orders

"... [W]e the Inhabitants and Residents ... now cohabiting and dwelling in and upon the River of Connectecotte and the lands thereunto adjoining; and well knowing where a people are gathered together the word of God requires that to maintain the peace ... there should be an orderly and decent Government established ..."

The above statement, taken from the beginning of the Fundamental Orders, says that the people living in Connecticut are required by their faith to keep the peace. To keep that peace, they will create a government.

Charles II was king of England from 1660 until 1685. He gave a royal charter to the Connecticut Colony in 1661. Inset: The Fundamental Orders said that the authority of a government comes from the consent of the people it governs.

Early Government

Most of the 13 colonies were started with a **charter**. The Connecticut settlers, however, did not have permission from the king, Charles I, to settle there. In 1639, the leaders of the Connecticut Colony created their own government by writing the Fundamental Orders.

In 1661, John Winthrop Jr., the governor of Connecticut, received a charter from Charles II, which secured the colony's right to make its own laws. For many years **Parliament** and Britain's king argued about how much power Colonial governments should have. This would soon cause problems between the colonies and Britain.

Connecticut made the Puritan church, called the Congregational Church, the colony's official church. Settlers paid taxes to provide for the church. Colonists were also expected to attend church. Few settlers in Connecticut lived more than 6 miles (9.7 km) from a church. Yale College, shown above, was founded in 1701 to train preachers for the Congregational Church.

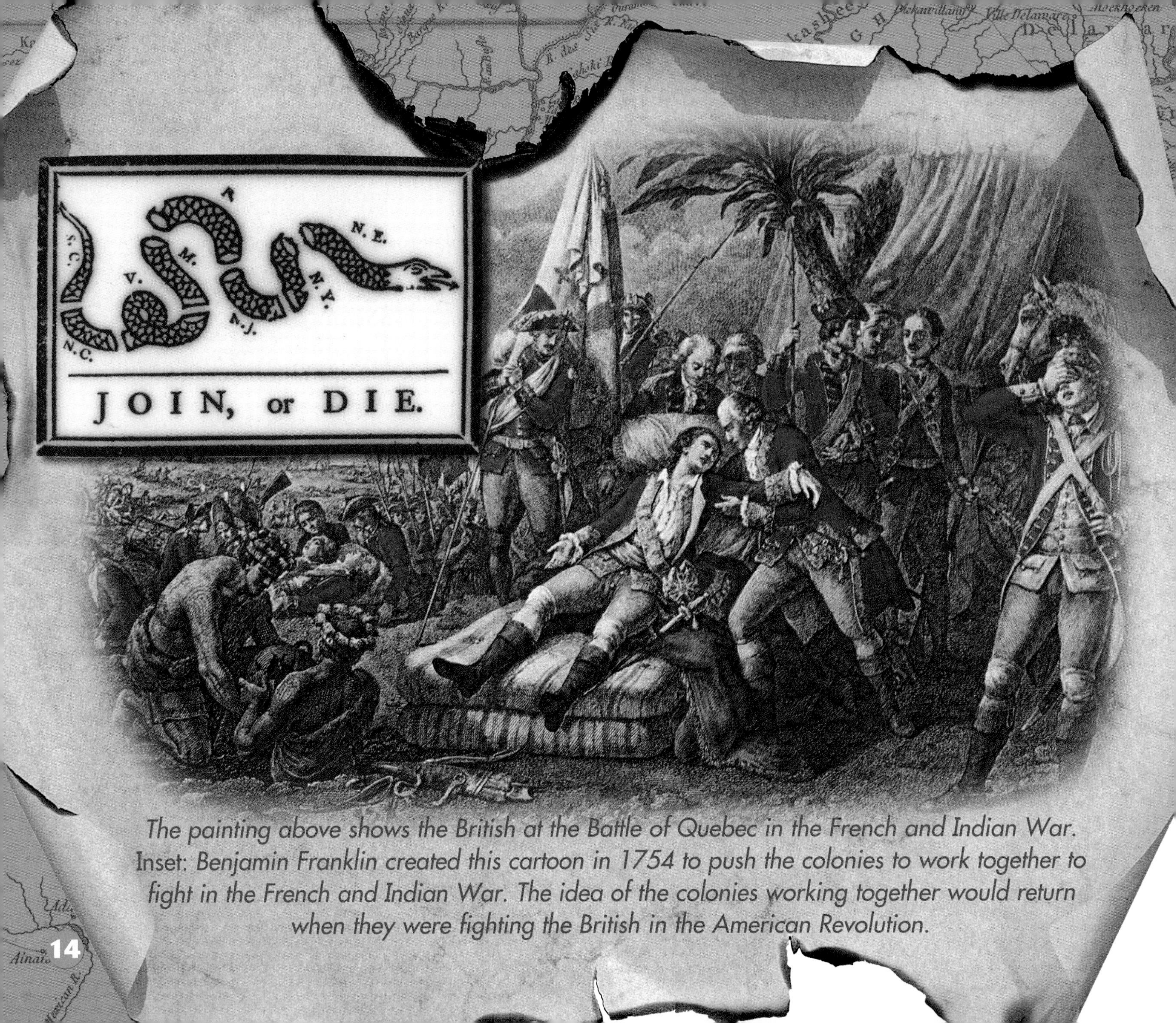

The painting above shows the British at the Battle of Quebec in the French and Indian War. Inset: *Benjamin Franklin created this cartoon in 1754 to push the colonies to work together to fight in the French and Indian War. The idea of the colonies working together would return when they were fighting the British in the American Revolution.*

Britain Tries to Take Control

Until the mid-1700s, the British were often too busy fighting wars with other countries or dealing with problems in their own country to take much part in affairs in their North American colonies. That changed after the **French and Indian War**.

The British won the war in 1763. It was a very expensive war for Britain. Because the war was fought in North America, the British wanted the colonists to help pay for it. The British also wanted to make sure they got a share of the colonies' earnings, such as those from Connecticut's factories. They wanted more control over the colonies' governments, also. Now that they were not in danger of attack by the French, the colonies began to feel less dependent on the British. Britain decided it needed to tighten its control over the colonies.

The cartoon above shows colonists protesting the Stamp Act. The poster one of the colonists holds reads, "England's Folly & America's Ruin." That means that England's mistake is hurting the colonies. Inset: This is a half-penny stamp that was used under the Stamp Act on a taxed paper product.

Connecticut Protests

In 1765, Parliament passed a new tax on paper goods called the Stamp Act. The Assembly of Connecticut wrote a letter to Parliament to protest, or object to, the tax. It stated that under Britain's laws, British subjects paid taxes that they had approved by electing the officials who passed the taxes. Connecticut did not elect officials to represent, or speak for, them in Parliament. To protest the new rules and taxes, the colonists refused to buy English goods.

Settlers in Connecticut and other colonies formed groups called the Sons of Liberty to fight the Stamp Act. The Stamp Act was repealed in 1766, but Parliament passed other unfair taxes and laws. The more the colonists protested, the more Britain tried to force them to obey.

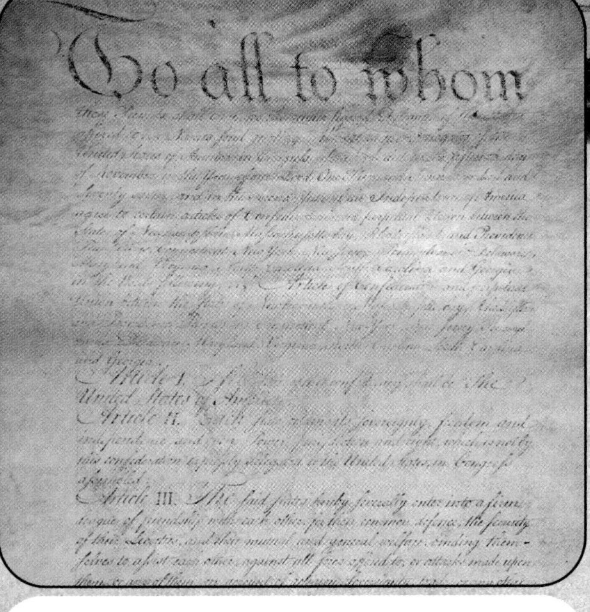
To all to whom

Article II. Each state retains its sovereignty, freedom and independence, and every Power, Jurisdiction and right, which is not by this confederation expressly delegated to the United States, in Congress assembled.

Article III. The said states hereby severally enter into a firm league of friendship with each other, for their common defence, the security of their Liberties, and their mutual and general welfare, binding themselves to assist each other, against all force offered to, or attacks made upon

From the Articles of Confederation

"II. Each state retains its sovereignty, freedom, and independence . . ."

"III. The said States hereby severally enter into a firm league of friendship with each other, for their common defense . . ."

The first of these two statements from the Articles of Confederation says that the colonies, now called states, are separate from one another. The next statement says that these states are working together to guard themselves and each other from Britain.

The painting above shows members of the First Continental Congress meeting in Philadelphia, Pennsylvania, in 1774. Inset: *The Articles of Confederation was a set of laws that the states followed during the American Revolution. It was signed in 1777 and ratified, or approved, in 1781.*

The Colonies Work Together

On September 5, 1774, leaders from the 13 colonies met at the **Continental Congress** in Philadelphia, Pennsylvania. Connecticut sent Joseph Platt Cooke, Silas Deane, Eliphalet Dyer, and Roger Sherman. The Congress sent letters of protest to King George III.

In July 1776, a year after the start of the **American Revolution**, the Continental Congress met again. On July 4, the **Declaration of Independence** was signed. The colonies agreed to work together to fight the British and wrote the **Articles of Confederation**, a set of laws that governed the colonies during the Revolution.

In 1776, Congress secretly sent Connecticut shopkeeper Silas Deane to France. He was sent to ask the French for help in the war. They agreed to secretly lend money to the colonies to pay for the war. The French also sent officers to help the colonists fight starting in 1778.

In the painting above, privateers are being hired in New London. In return for attacking British ships, privateers were allowed to keep the ships' contents. Inset: *Benedict Arnold changed sides to fight for the British. He led an attack on Virginia in the fall of 1780, and in 1781, he led an attack on New London, Connecticut.*

Connecticut in the American Revolution

Although most of the important battles in the Revolution were fought outside Connecticut, the people of Connecticut still played an important role in the war. More than 200 American **privateers** sailed from Connecticut. They interrupted British shipping and guarded the American coast from British attack. Many men from Connecticut also joined the Continental army.

Benedict Arnold was a Continental army general who later changed sides to fight for the British. Jonathan Trumbull, of Lebanon, Connecticut, served as one of George Washington's most-trusted advisers. Nathan Hale, of Coventry, went on a secret mission to discover the British army's plans. Hale was captured and hanged. His famous last words were, "I **regret** that I have but one life to lose for my country."

The Connecticut Compromise

The American Revolution officially ended in 1783. The new nation had to pay back the money owed to the countries from which it had borrowed money. Under the Articles of Confederation, the United States' government had no power to collect taxes to repay this money. The articles did not provide a way for the states to work together as a country.

In May 1787, the Colonial leaders met in Philadelphia to form a new set of rules. Each state had a different idea about how the states should be represented. Connecticut representative Roger Sherman suggested a compromise, or agreement, which proposed a **bicameral legislature**. All the states agreed on this plan. On January 9, 1788, Connecticut approved the **Constitution** and became the fifth state.

Glossary

American Revolution (uh-MER-uh-ken reh-vuh-LOO-shun) Battles that soldiers from the American colonies fought against Britain for freedom, from 1775 to 1783.

Articles of Confederation (AR-tih-kulz UV kun-feh-deh-RAY-shun) The laws that governed the United States before the Constitution was created.

bicameral legislature (by-KAM-rul LEH-jis-lay-chur) A law-making body consisting of two parts, such as the Senate and the House of Representatives in the U.S. Congress.

charter (CHAR-tur) An official agreement giving someone permission to do something.

Constitution (kohn-stih-TOO-shun) The basic rules by which the United States is governed.

Continental Congress (kon-tih-NEN-tul KON-gres) A group, made up of a few people from every colony, that made decisions for the colonies.

Declaration of Independence (deh-kluh-RAY-shun UV in-duh-PEN-dints) An official announcement signed on July 4, 1776, in which American colonists stated they were free of British rule.

French and Indian War (FRENCH AND IN-dee-un WOR) The battles fought between 1754 and 1763 by England, France, and Native Americans for control of North America.

investment (in-VEST-ment) Money put into something, such as a company, in the hope of getting more money later on.

Parliament (PAR-lih-mint) The group in England that makes the country's laws.

privateers (pry-vuh-TEERZ) Sailors on armed ships allowed by a government to attack enemy ships.

regret (rih-GRET) To feel sorry about doing something.

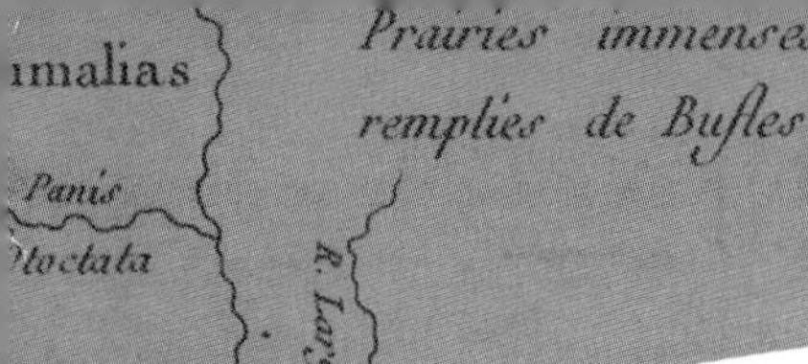

Index

Primary Sources

Page 4. Map of Long Island Sound. Circa 1679, Robbarte Ryder, John Carter Brown Library, Brown University, Providence, Rhode Island. **Page 6. Inset.** *John Winthrop, Jr.* (detail). Oil on canvas painting, circa 17th century, Sir Peter Lely, Massachusetts Historical Society, Boston, Massachusetts. **Page 8.** Pequot fort, Mystic, Connecticut (detail). 1638, John Underhill, from his book *Newes from America.* Mashantucket Pequot Museum and Research Center, Mashantucket, Connecticut. **Page 10. Inset.** Underhill family coat of arms. 1638, John Underhill, from the title page of his book *Newes from America.* New York Public Library. **Page 12. Inset.** First page of Fundamental Orders of Connecticut. 1639, Connecticut State Library, Hartford, Connecticut. **Page 13. Inset.** Yale College. Engraving, 1764, Kean Collection, New Haven, Connecticut. **Page 14. Inset.** *Join or Die.* Woodcut, May 9, 1754, Benjamin Franklin, Library of Congress, Washington, D.C. **Page 16. Inset.** Stamp Act tax stamp. 1764, reproduced in *Harper's Magazine*, June 1901. **Page 18.** *The First Continental Congress, Carpenter's Hall, Pennsylvania.* Oil on canvas painting, circa 18th century, Clyde O. Deland, Atwater Kent Museum of Philadelphia. **Page 18. Inset.** Articles of Confederation (first page). 1777, National Archives and Records Administration.

Web Sites

Due to the changing nature of Internet links, PowerKids Press has developed an online list of Web sites related to the subject of this book. This site is updated regularly. Please use this link to access the list:
http://www.powerkidslinks.com/pstclc/connect/